Bible Classics

David and Goliath

Modern Publishing
A Division of Unisystems, Inc.
New York, New York 10022
Series UPC: 39440

Long ago, there lived a good man named Samuel. He was a prophet of God.

God told Samuel to choose a man named Saul to be King of Israel. At first, King Saul was a good ruler but then he disobeyed God's commands.

Samuel loved King Saul, but he was sad because Saul had not listened to God. God told Samuel to find a new king.

Samuel went to see a man named Jesse. God would choose one of Jesse's sons to be the new king.

Jesse had eight sons. He brought seven of them to meet Samuel.
One by one, God turned down each son.

Finally Samuel asked Jesse, "Don't you have another son?" Jesse answered, "Yes, I do. My youngest son, David, is with our sheep out in the hills."

Samuel told Jesse to get the boy.

David was a good shepherd and a good musician. Many of his words are recorded in the Book of Psalms.

God told Samuel that this boy would one day be king of Israel. Samuel gave David a special blessing and then returned home.

Meanwhile, King Saul was unhappy being king. The spirit of God had left him and he could not rest. He decided to have someone play music to comfort him. When he heard about David's songs, Saul asked David to come and play for him.

Then there came a war with the Philistines. King Saul had to call for an army.

David's brothers joined Saul's army, but David was still too young. He went back to care for his father's sheep.

The Israelites were afraid because the Philistine army had one very big and very strong soldier. His name was Goliath. He was so tall he looked like a giant.

No man in the army, not even King Saul, dared to fight Goliath. King Saul asked his strongest soldiers to try, but they were all too scared.

One day, David went to visit his brothers. They told him about Goliath.

"If no one else will go, then I will fight this enemy," he said.

The soldiers brought David before King Saul. David said, "The Lord will save me from this enemy, for I will fight for the Lord and His people."

King Saul told one of his soldiers to put the king's own armor on David. But Saul's armor was much too big for David.

David decided to use his sling and picked up five smooth stones from a nearby brook. When Goliath saw David, he just laughed.

Goliath couldn't believe that this boy wanted to fight him. Still, David knew that God would help him.

David chose one smooth stone from his pouch. He took careful aim and slung the stone at Goliath.

The stone struck Goliath square on the forehead with a loud *thwack,* and he fell with a crash.

David had trusted in the Lord and he won.

When Goliath's army saw the giant soldier fall, they ran away in fear. King Saul was very proud of David.

The king's soldiers called David a hero and celebrated his victory over Goliath.

David lived a long life. When he grew up, he became the king of Israel.

David is remembered as one of the greatest kings of all time, for he was blessed with the spirit of the Lord.